T0065552

RUMI
IN MY HEAD

JOAN COFRANCESCO

authorHOUSE®

AuthorHouse™
1663 Liberty Drive
Bloomington, IN 47403
www.authorhouse.com
Phone: 1 (800) 839-8640

Published by AuthorHouse 08/24/2016

ISBN: 978-1-5246-2659-4 (sc)
ISBN: 978-1-5246-2677-8 (e)

stray kittens

not in love
don't have a van gogh
don't have a cat
all i have are
images
stumbling around
in my head
like stray kittens

putting on the dog

across hardwood floors
our fat cat struts proudly
like buddha himself

round sandlewood beads
tibetan rosaries
beneath the cat's white paws

my cabin
a black monastery
i study
        eastern poets
  i ching
        until the moon
signals me like
        a bell
        to bed

vacation

bring me back
a t-shirt

i'll watch your cats
and sit by a tree
reading a book
of love poems

watching sea horses float
around in the tank
you bought me
i wonder if the button
is still missing from
your flannel shirt
and if you still wear my
indian beaded belt
on your jeans

syracuse sunday
the herald covered with snow
three crows on the line

we're naked
tangled together
wrapped in scifi

you tell me
i'm not living
i need to travel

my hands move
on your hair
back & thighs

calligraphy II

i am brushstroking
a cat
chanting the mantras
of my life

after the orgy

i go home
to an empty room
over dom's grocery store

watching the light
between the cat's whiskers
dying
of unwritten poems

black cat beside me
which one of us
smoked a joint

how far is
across the room
so many books
and cats

tantric massage
i am wet clay

eucharist
rosaries
tibetan beads
where am i now

lions
stare at me
as i walk
up the stairs
of the nyc
public library

coffee
cherrywood
goya's paintings
nightmares
last night

mr softie
is a jingle truck
down all the streets
of my life

cheap port wine
no better friend
than kerouac

wait
the coming of spring
boats
poets
she-cats
in heat

young muscular boys
in the taverns and baths
michaelangelo's muse

stretched out
on the bed
with big orange cat
bob
both of us
listening
to the rain

i am a flicker
watching the fire

reverdy
o'hara
brautigan
talking to each other
in my backpack
on a train
to nyc

i prefer
the snakes
of modigliani
to the mammals
of the renaissance

moving thru rain
on a train
french poetry
beer
thinking only about
this morning
warm

getting up at 3
to paint
or read
or look at the moon
retirement
wonder
life

hear the weathervane squeaking
can't sleep
lift weights
whirl like a dervish
masturbate until
there's nothing left
but this poem

it's a lonely
college campus
new york times   coffeeshop
wandering among trees cement
young couple laughing
sunday

tubman

it's about time
they put a woman
from my home town
auburn
on a bill

smell
leather
feel your sweat
believe me
i have no regrets
about our fucking
subway ride

black tie shirt
silver chain
tight jeans
& brooklyn swagger

van gogh
to his bro theo:
the sadness

she was a clerk
read hemingway
dostoevsky
drank gin
straight

sitting with a guinness
on a pier
in nyc
breezy spring

i'm in the dead cat position
but my siamese always
wants to play

found in a cookie
after eating moo shu chicken

there is
no such thing
as an
ordinary
cat

wrestling
with my shadow
and it's a draw

wandering piazza
san marco venice
listening to vivaldi
surrounded by pigeons
and being fed
poems

as a kid
i wanted to be
an artist
but i hated the smell
of paint and turpentine
so i became
an artist of words

reading poetry
drinking wine
by the fire
6 purring cats
on persian rugs
the hours

three days
incense
candles
writing
balling
pizza boxes
cat sitting
with its back to us

your
naked
leg over
stickley chair
exposing
black
and red
silk underwear
it doesn't
get any
better
than
this

on slack mattress
rumpled sheets
her perverse whisperings
electrocute me

rainy nyc day
i go
to the met museum
to see etruscan jewelry
then go home
to my cats
ted and sylvia

long brown hair
leather jacket
turquoise

the smell of patchouli
on my orange cat's
fur
after she left

in the piazza
accordion music plays
an italian woman
drinking tuscan wine
smiles at me
what else is there

cell phones
taking over

walking
playing
books
gone
only pharmaceuticals
and darkness

she wore
a tibetan
skullnecklace
i liked
having her
around me

last night i dreamt
a drone flying over me
again and again
and i lifted my shirt up
flashing my tits at it
each time

after snuggling
i want to paint
fireworks
on my chelsea lover's toes
while she sleeps away
the after-
noon

my list of favorites
lake ponchartrain
larry rivers
basquait
and your ass

try to study byron
when young girls
with long brown hair
keep knocking
on your dorm door
and saying
let's go out for a beer

reading
li po
rice wine
mountains
yellow river
free
and happy

a hot summer night
in fort hill cemetery
seward, tubman, case

every wednesday

red and black
lace panties
for me
to rip off

the anger of
BOMB is
corso-ing
through me

cat purring
on the couch
how i feel
when you come home

looking at a tucker
over the moon
i realize
how abstract i am

no belongings
but my backpack bones
i wander
and i breathe

annual
blood
mammogram
urine
pap smear
x-rays
echocardiogram
and doctor's lecture

my cat
will not accept
a yankees baseball
cap

let's cuddle
under my cat quilt
we can
stack
wood
later

watching you
put on your lipstick
i have no ambition

i have trouble
when people
or cats die
and religion is
no help

cavafy
desire
for young naked
greek men
fueling his poems

i love symbols
$$^(*&)+_+
precisely because
i don't understand them

i sit in the kitchen
thinking up psalms
for fish bones
chicken bones
walnut shells
and the table

i write most of my poems
at 3 am
can't sleep
cats prowling
xanax
wine
moonlight
candles
the velvet
underground

to lie
in bed all day with you
snow glistening
woodstove glowing

sax seduction sanborn sex
hot fudge
sunday

gregorian chants
strings chimes gongs
cleansing

sweating
reeking of brandy
after skiing
we fucked
through bolero

2am
reading
turtle island
my cat bowie
sleeping beside me
coltrane playing
my retirement

zen of antiquing

fall
in the leather seat
of the polished red mg
hood gleaming
engine purring
along route 20
nothing better than this

lying
with my 2 cats
ulysses
and penelope
i look up
at my skylight
half moon
4 stars
venus

retirement
snowing outside
i'm listening to smokey
eating banana
pancakes
it's just me
and my imagination

gathering lavender
in tuscany
to put in my suitcase
essential oils

in my parents' old house
fingering yearbooks
and records
janis
roach clip
turquoise ring
in my own drunken boat

sipping
merlot sultry
dinah washington

like my black cat
heating his fur
in the sunlight
by the window

i am comfortable
with my ghosts

high with you
after a hot fudge sundae
the soft sax
your warm tongue
between my legs

sidewalks
covered with snow
i should shovel
but the cherrywood
fire glows and smells
almost as wonderful
as your soft skin
in my bed

i love to watch her
take a bath
skylight sunshine
on her skin

wandering
the ancient
streets
of rome
i feel like
audrey hepburn
in *roman holiday*
searching
for the
trevi
fountain

rainy afternoon
we talk about
movies poetry
kierkegaard
cardiology
two childless women
one orange cat

i have become
a hermit

    my life
      three cats

Printed in the United States
By Bookmasters